Spotlight on the
MAYA, AZTEC, and INCA CIVILIZATIONS

Ancient INCA TECHNOLOGY

Ryan Nagelhout

PowerKiDS press.

NEW YORK

Published in 2017 by The Rosen Publishing Group, Inc.
29 East 21st Street, New York, NY 10010

Editor: Sarah Machajewski
Designer: Reann Nye

Photo Credits: Cover kccullenPhoto/Shutterstock.com; pp.4, 10 https://commons.wikimedia.org/wiki/File-Inca_Empire.svg; p. 5 saiko3p/Shutterstock.com; pp. 7, 13 Glowimages/Getty Images; pp. 8, 9 Byelikova Oksana/Shutterstock.com; p. 11 Pola Damonte/Shutterstock.com; p. 12 https://en.wikipedia.org/wiki/File:Conchamarka_(cooking_stove_spot).jpg; p. 15 HUGHES Herve/hemis.fr/Getty Images; p. 17 Science & Society Picture Library/SSPL/Getty Images; p. 19 chris kolaczan/Shutterstock.com; p. 20 RIRF Stock/Shutterstock.com; p. 21 ckchiu/Shutterstock.com; p. 23 obscur/Shutterstock.com; p. 24 Cecilia Alvarenga/Getty Images; p. 25 DEA / G. DAGLI ORTI/De Agostini Picture Library/Getty Images; p. 27 China Photos/Getty Images News/Getty Images; p. 29 Ira Block/National Geographic/Getty Images.

Cataloging-in-Publication Data

Names: Nagelhout, Ryan.
Title: Ancient Inca technology / Ryan Nagelhout.
Description: New York : PowerKids Press, 2017. | Series: Spotlight on the Maya, Aztec, and Inca civilizations | Includes index.
Identifiers: ISBN 9781499419535 (pbk.) | ISBN 9781499419566 (library bound) | ISBN 9781499419542 (6 pack)
Subjects: LCSH: Incas--Juvenile literature. | Incas--History--Juvenile literature. | Incas--Antiquities--Juvenile literature.
Classification: LCC F3429.N34 2017 | DDC 985'.019--dc23

CPSIA Compliance Information: Batch #BS16PK: For further information contact Rosen Publishing, New York, New York at 1-800-237-9932.

CONTENTS

THE CIVILIZATION OF SCIENCE

The Inca were a **culture** of people who ruled much of present-day South America from around 1200 to 1533. Millions of people lived under Inca rule in an empire that stretched thousands of miles along the western coast of South America.

The Inca were easily conquered by the Spanish, and they left no written records. These factors may make some people think the Inca were primitive. However, the Inca developed amazing technology in many different fields. Scientists studying the Inca have uncovered **complex** cities, amazing roadways, medical skills, and **unique** farming methods that allowed the Inca Empire to flourish and grow. Much of this technology was hidden for centuries, but today we have a much better understanding of how people living in the Inca Empire used technology to improve their lives.

These ruins at Ollantaytambo in southern Peru are evidence of Inca technology, which is the use of science to solve problems. Even without modern tools, the Inca used science to achieve many technological marvels.

BUILDING AN EMPIRE

The Inca city of Cuzco is located in the Andes Mountains of modern-day Peru. The Inca built amazing structures there using ideas they developed or borrowed from cultures they conquered.

Inca stonemasons carved huge, heavy stones to fit tightly together, much like pieces of a puzzle. Modern **architects** believe they have figured out how the Inca managed to shape the stones so perfectly. Small rocks have been found at the **quarries** where the Inca mined their large rocks. Originally found in riverbeds, these black stones were used to smooth the edges of larger rocks until they fit perfectly together. This method may be one reason why some Inca structures still stand today, having survived centuries of earthquakes.

Common people usually lived in simple homes with just one story and one room. The walls were made of mud, and the roof was made of woven plant material.

Inca stonemasons built their structures without using mortar, or a binder, to hold the stones together. You can see how perfectly the stones fit in the remains of this temple near Cuzco.

SACSAYHUAMÁN

Sacsayhuamán was a fortress built to protect Cuzco, the Inca capital city. Today, all that's left are three zigzagging stone walls. The Killke people built sections of the walls around 1100, but the Inca expanded them. Much construction took place under emperor Pachacuti Inca Yupanqui, whose reign began around 1438.

Historians estimate more than 30,000 men worked almost 30 years to build Sacsayhuamán. Laborers had to transport rock from quarries far from Cuzco. They were able to pry the heavy rocks free with bronze tools.

Sacsayhuamán had three layers of stone walls to protect it. Much of the building was taken apart by the Spanish when they conquered the Inca in the 16th century.

Some stones were as tall as 29 feet (8.8 m) and weighed up to 360 tons (326.6 mt). With no animals, wheeled carts, or other methods to help move the stones, the Inca built ramps with dirt. Logs tied to ropes made of leather and reeds helped them move the rocks up high slopes. These methods show how the Inca were able to adapt to their surroundings, using available resources to build and protect an empire.

CONNECTING IT ALL

The Inca roads are a great feat of engineering and an example of how the government used its people as a tool. Citizens of the empire were required to perform a labor service for a certain amount of time during the year. This was called *mit'a*. *Mit'a* labor built a **network** of roads called Qhapaq Ñan, which covered about 18,641 miles (30,000 km).

The Royal Road was one of the highway system's main routes. It stretched nearly 4,000 miles (6,437 km), running through Quito in present-day Ecuador, traveling through Cajamarca and Cuzco, and ending near Tucumán, Argentina. Another main roadway ran 3,000 miles (4,828 km) from the Gulf of Guayaquil in present-day Ecuador to the Maule River in Chile.

Long stretches of the Inca road network still survive today in six countries: Argentina, Bolivia, Chile, Colombia, Ecuador, and Peru.

Many other roads connected these two main paths, linking cities and making sure every part of the empire could be reached. The roads were narrow because the Inca didn't have the wheel, so they didn't need to make space for wagons or carts.

The roads closest to Cuzco were the most frequently used. They were widest and paved with stone. Parts of the roads that traveled through the steep mountains were built to create a level route, making the journey easier on travelers. Bridges helped the Inca cross rivers and **ravines**.

The Inca measured distances by placing large stones on the side of the road to serve as distance markers. Rest houses, called *tampus*, were located along the roads. *Tampus* had food and supplies for travelers, as well as areas for their animals to rest. *Tampus* were protected by stone walls and built from resources in the **environment**.

Troops and, with permission, people moving goods were allowed to travel the road system.

Common people weren't allowed to travel on the roads. They were only for government and military use. Fast messengers called *chasquis* ran between certain points to relay messages. Together, the *chasquis* could run about 250 miles (402 km) a day.

BRIDGES AND ROPES

Inca roads climbed through mountains and crossed plains, and they even went through tunnels of rock. The roads also ran across rivers and streams with the help of some amazing bridges. The Inca built suspension bridges, which are bridges with overhead cables supporting the roadway.

These bridges were made of plant materials—including vines, branches, and a grass called ichu—which were braided together for strength. The braided ropes were used as the bridge's walkway and supports. Each side of the bridge had a wooden or stone tower to which the ropes were secured.

Inca bridges could hold thousands of pounds, and some may have stretched more than 150 feet (46 m)—longer than any European bridge built around the same time. Sometimes, suspended baskets called *oroya* were an alternative to bridges. Large enough for two or three people, the baskets carried travelers across the gap.

There may have been more than 200 suspension bridges like this one throughout the Inca Empire. Villagers replace this bridge, which crosses the Apurímac River, every year!

QUIPUS

One of the most important inventions in Inca society was the quipu. A quipu is a device made of strings and knots. Quipus have one main string with knotted strings attached to it. Without a written language, quipus were the way the Inca government kept track of the movement of people, goods, and messages.

Certain knots were used to represent numbers, and the position of the knot represented a base unit such as 1, 10, or 100. The color of the quipu likely represented the type of good that was being counted, such as gold or crops from a harvest. Quipus also recorded taxes and kept track of *mit'a* labor requirements.

Though they were used quite often, not all Inca knew how to use them. Only special officials, called *quipucamayocs*, were trained to use quipus. However, each *quipucamayoc* had his own system, and the information could not be written down. For this reason, it's hard for us to know what quipus mean just by looking at them.

The Inca created quipu strings from llama or alpaca hair or from cotton plants.

CORICANCHA, TEMPLE OF THE SUN

Coricancha was the Inca's temple of the sun. The city of Cuzco may have been built in the shape of a puma, which is a large cat. Coricancha was located where the puma's tail would be. This is also where four main roads came together. More than 4,000 priests lived in the temple, which was the most sacred place in the city.

Coricancha may have functioned as a calendar for the Inca. Stones placed in the foothills of the Andes could be seen from the temple, and their shadows marked the **solstices** and **equinoxes** the Inca observed. The temple had four rooms that honored the god or goddess of the moon, stars, thunder, and rainbows. One room contained a giant gold disc that was placed to catch the sunlight. During the summer solstice, the sunlight lit an area where only the emperor was allowed to sit.

The Spanish destroyed much of Coricancha. They built a Catholic cathedral over it when they took control of Cuzco.

SPANISH CATHEDRAL
CORICANCHA

BUILDING THE FARM

Most citizens of the Inca Empire were farmers. They lived in communities called ayllus, and each ayllu was responsible for growing the food it needed. Farmers kept a portion of the food they grew. The rest was given to the Inca emperor, who directed the government to store it, and priests, who used the food in religious ceremonies.

INCA TERRACES NEAR YANQUE, PERU

It's estimated the terraces covered about 2.47 million acres (1 million hectares) of land in the Inca Empire.

Inca farmers grew potatoes, corn, and quinoa, which is a seed. Because they lived in the steep mountains, the Inca had to make their own flat land on which to grow crops. They did this by carving the mountains themselves. Called terraces, these level steps provided flat land for farming.

The Inca developed a way of freeze-drying their food, which helped it last longer. This process involved putting a cloth over the food, leaving it outside to freeze, and stepping on it to get rid of extra water. Chuños, or freeze-dried potatoes, were made this way.

THE WATER WAY

Water was an important resource for the Inca. They developed several ways of moving it to the places that needed it. Terraces helped farmers **irrigate** their crops. Water would move through terraces and could be diverted, or moved in a different direction, by rock formations. Terraces also worked to collect water, which was helpful during **droughts**.

The Inca also built aqueducts, which moved water from sources that were many miles away from cities. At Machu Picchu, for example, a channel 820 yards (750 m) long, 4.7 inches (12 cm) deep, and 5.9 inches (15 cm) wide brought water to the mountain city.

Before building a settlement, the Inca probably studied nearby water sources to see how much the flow and amount of water changed during the year. Then, Inca builders got to work making a stable, secure foundation for a settlement. Proper drainage was an important part of this process.

Today, many Inca canals and terraces sit unused, but some Peruvians are working to restore them.

WEAPONS OF WAR

The Inca used a variety of tools. They used small stones and bronze tools to shape the stones used in their structures. When fishing, they used nets, spears, and copper hooks. However, they didn't have one tool that helped many civilizations develop: the wheel.

Some of the Inca's most fascinating tools are the ones used in war. Soldiers used wooden and bronze swords and axes. They also used bronze and stone clubs. These weapons were strong enough to break an enemy's bones. Slings called *huaracas* were used to toss small rocks at high speeds. One account from the Spanish said one shot was able to break a sword in half from 100 feet (30.5 m) away.

STATUE OF PACHACUTI, NINTH INCA EMPEROR

In this engraving, Inca soldiers take on the Spanish who invaded their empire.

Shields were made of wood, wicker, or deerskins, and had a cloth apron that was meant to protect soldiers' legs. Warriors wore a shield of hard chonta wood around their neck to protect their back. Without iron, the Inca tipped their weapons with stone, copper, bone, or fire-hardened wood.

CUTTING INTO THE HEAD

Archaeologists digging near Inca ruins have found skulls with holes in them. Many argued that the holes were injuries suffered through war, but recently scientists discovered they came from doctors performing surgery! It was likely used to help people with head injuries, such as the kind suffered in battle. The surgery—called trepanation—removes a part of the skull to relieve pressure caused by a buildup of fluid.

The idea of skull surgery without modern tools may seem scary, but Inca healers avoided cutting areas of the skull that could cause harm to the brain or more bleeding. This shows that Inca healers probably understood the makeup of the head and brain very well.

Surprisingly, most surgery sites didn't get **infected**, according to scientists. Scientists reported that balsam and plants that had soap-like properties were used to keep infections from setting in. Wild plants were also used to treat pain. Coca, wild tobacco, and a beer-like drink called *chicha* helped patients feel better.

Scientists have determined that this skull belonged to an Inca woman who lived 500 years ago.

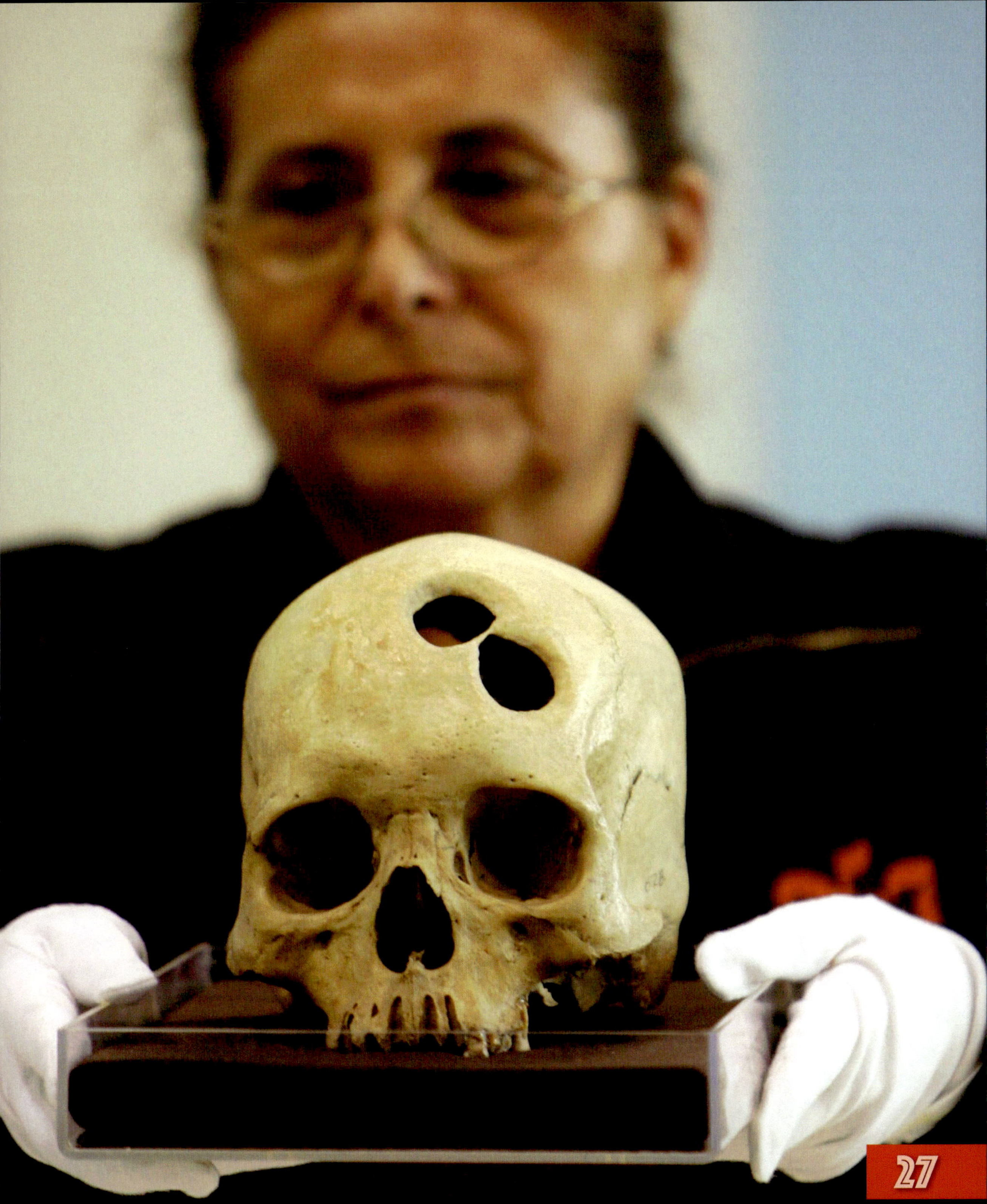

DEAD TECHNOLOGY

Death wasn't the end for the Inca. The Inca mummified some of their most important people. A mummy is a dead body preserved through a special process. In the coastal area of ancient Chile and Peru, the Chinchorro people, a pre-Inca culture, removed the skin, brain, and organs of the dead. The bones were dried with ash and the body was put back together with twigs and animal skin, if needed.

Some Inca mummies were once people who were the victims of human sacrifice. They were killed to gain favor from Inca gods. Their bodies were wrapped in cotton and allowed to dry naturally. Mummies were often buried with valuables, including clothing, food, and weapons.

The Ice Maiden is a famous Inca mummy. One of the most well-preserved mummies in the world, the teenage girl was killed in a **ritual** sacrifice around 500 years ago. The cold temperatures in the frozen region of the Andes kept bacteria from growing on the body, which is what would cause it to decay.

The Inca honored their kings even after those kings became mummies. The Spanish, who saw this as a threat to their rule, seized many royal mummies when they conquered the Inca.

THE QUICK END

The Inca Empire fell quickly with the arrival of the Spanish, led by Francisco Pizarro. Sicknesses such as smallpox killed natives quickly, and Pizarro killed the Inca's leaders and marched on their roads to conquer Cuzco in 1533. By 1572, the empire had completely fallen.

Though their culture and much of their history were lost in the conquest, the Inca left a lasting impact on South America. Their roads, temples, and even their mummies were built to last. Ruins of important buildings still stand today, and millions of people visit the ancient city of Machu Picchu to learn more about the fascinating Inca culture.

The Inca accomplished amazing things without modern tools or the wheel. Their network of roads, use of quipus to save information, and advanced medical techniques such as skull surgery illustrate a fascinating history centuries after the empire's collapse.

GLOSSARY

architect (AAR-kuh-tehkt): A person who designs buildings and aids in their construction.

complex (kahm-PLEKS): Made of many parts.

culture (KUHL-chur): The customs and ways of life of a society.

drought (DROWT): A period of time marked by little rain.

environment (ihn-VY-ruhn-munt): The surroundings in which a person lives.

equinox (EE-kwuh-nahks): Either of the two times in a year when day and night are the same length.

infected (in-FEHK-tihd): Having to do with an illness caused by harmful organisms, or germs.

irrigate (EER-uh-gayt): To supply water to land or crops.

network (NET-werk): A system of related or connected parts.

quarry (KWOR-ee): An open pit used to dig up stones.

ravine (ruh-VEEN): A deep, narrow gorge with steep sides.

ritual (RIH-chuh-wuhl): A religious ceremony performed through a series of repeated steps.

solstice (SOHL-stuhs): Either of the two times in a year when the sun is highest or lowest in the sky at noon, marking the longest and shortest days.

unique (yoo-NEEK): Unusual or one of a kind.

INDEX

PRIMARY SOURCE LIST

Cover: Ruins at Ollantaytambo. Built by the Inca. Stone and earth. 15th century. Located near Cuzco, Peru.

Page 7: Ruins of the Inca Temple of the Moon. Built by the Inca. Stone. Date unknown. Located near Cuzco, Peru.

Pages 8–9: Ruins at Sacsayhuamán. Built by the Killke people and expanded by the Inca. Stone. ca. 1100. Located near Cuzco, Peru.

Page 25: Inca army attacking the Spanish. Created by Felipe Guaman Poma de Ayala. Published in *The First New Chronicle and Good Government*. Engraving. 1612–1615. Now kept in The Royal Library, Copenhagen, Denmark.

WEBSITES

Due to the changing nature of Internet links, PowerKids Press has developed an online list of websites related to the subject of this book. This site is updated regularly. Please use this link to access the list: www.powerkidslinks.com/soac/inct